In Essence

Nasreen Hussain

BookLeaf Publishing

Presentation by *BookLeaf Publishing*

Web: www.bookleafpub.com

E-mail: info@bookleafpub.com

ISBN: 978-93-95784-33-7

First edition 2022

DEDICATION

Father. Until we meet again.

ACKNOWLEDGEMENT

God, the most High.

PREFACE

Riding on the winds of change, counting on the wings of grace.

Gifts

I used to care about so many things
I used to care what people think
Whether some ships
Would float or sink

Now sometimes I think its better
Just to let some sail
To let them go

Whether or not they come back to shore
Is what determines life

In this test of time
In this dream against all odds
In this fight against the self
In this struggle to make sense

Why and the occasional how
Accepting things
Whatever change
However calm or sudden
You can't hide the truth
Or what's in your heart

Like your demons
The light likes to come out and play too
So let her
Don't resist her
Close your eyes and kiss her
Stay for a while
Until you feel whole again
And can make distinctions
Between excuses and reasons
To do or not

To run after dreams
To break one's heart
Sometimes you don't get to decide

Where I am now?

I climbed a hill
Only to find a mountain
And that's great
Cause sometimes I love a challenge

If that means
There is still room to grow
If that means
There is still room to experience
Than why not?

Take the young with the old
The song of life won't repeat itself
Unless you fail to change
Unless you fail to distinguish the lessons gained
And so here I am
Writing again
Only because it's a true form of listening

You have gifts
Use them.

Stricken

So much coming down
Mostly down my face
Proud and humble

Mixed bag of feelings
Gotta ask, whats next?

Letting go of whats coming?
Letting go of what did?

Being the beginning.
Where do you live?

Knowing who I was
Being who I am?
The space in between

What's my plan?

I don't know
But I'm driving

With that little
Trickle of faith

Enough to send me away
Finding that horizon

Then crossing it

Getting to a higher place

Realizing how
I only needed
A place
To jump down

Keep the faith.

A Double Edged Sword

This is life:

A double edged sword
What caused you relief today
May later cause you pain

On and on
Simplifying
Complicating
Necessary
Unnecessary

What are you trying to teach me?
That
Life
Goes
On

Nostaligia

Take me back to the place where I began, a place of stainless pleasure.

A time of hand-me-downs and days gone by, where sentences were sterile and lovely in their innocence.

Take me to the time of budding flowers, when motivation was something to be sought after–where the future still held all her stars in the sky.

Once in A While

One day
Once in a while
You won't care so much

Then life will ask you

If you love.

Vow

Between everything- we've got our lives to live.
We don't get to decide how long it is.
So let me love you, the best I can.
Even if life unfolds a different plan.
God put you in my path.
Let's walk together.
Make the road as we go.

I give you my life and I love you for everything:
Every feeling, every contrast and inhibition,
every knowing and transition.

I give you my life, the only life I have got to
give.
So thank you for being in it.

Waiting

What do you want?
What are you afraid of?
Have things come back around?
Do you hate it?
Is there something else
But can't say it?

Is there more to it than being crazy?
And yet its that same insanity
That preserves me

The way I live my life
Is an honest guess
And it kills me a little more each day
Whether as a prisoner in a cage
Whether as a bird catching air
Whether its a tear behind a veil

The more I learn the more I realize
I know nothing
And that's why I say
We are fools

Fools in love
Fools at work
Fools at play

Fools all waiting
For death some day.

Gasping for Breath

We watch sunsets go by from a distance
Lean on me
But don’t let it mean
More than you are willing to lose
And that goes for me too

Love takes courage
But I’m a fool
And I suck at forgiveness
When you’ve done all you can
Maybe it’s time to give things over

And move on
And carry on
As you keep your feet on the ground
As you tip toe across that dotted line
Keeping your gaze ahead
With no sign of anything

Just wind and air
Invisible mysteries
Passing through your lungs

You carry on with the balancing act
You inquire and question
Going back and forth in your head
And lose focus when you look down
But never question gasping for breath

Fumée

Smoking for me
is a nice distraction to keep
it doesn't make me feel guilty
and almost feels like a luxury
a choice I paid for
in my own breaths
and though I would never want to make a habit of it
or become an addict
it is still something I enjoy:

taking it out of its pack
rolling it up to my nose
taking a sniff
putting it to my lip
lighting it up
watching it smoke
every thought
whatever it was
didn't matter
as it did in the beginning
and with each puff
each silent puff,
life gets
a little
shorter

Change

Change life? Change inside?
To a person no less familiar than who you knew
all along?
Like tracing a finger over an old picture:
'I'm here to see you again. Maybe I'll stay longer,
maybe we can be friends. Maybe I'll surrender
and lessen the burdens of secrets, of ships sailed,
of light, of darkness, of heavens and hell.'

Now is all we have. No time wasted.
And every time my heart breaks... I get closer to
taking that trophy home.
'Why' is never a question so much a reason.

Slow Fade

It's over
So that it can begin.

Your pride
Is left with nothing.

By the time
you are out
of this time.

Life is a story
To say goodbye ~

Immersion

You are a reference point
of past
and
future dreaming

I am on my way
To some place
In the evening

An immersion
A gathering
In a draped gown of Crystal
Grinded into its fabric

I am walking through a forest
Incandescent
In the thick of it
A fortress

And the doors open
Sky magenta and magic
A spectacle and fountains
Ballet dancers playing with fire
And white horses
Wild without a harness

I walk into enchantment
Hundreds of eyes see me
But in this process
I am searching

The walls
Are mirrors
And I think I see
But the lights
Keep flickering

Your glimpses
Are not constant
In the flashes
I cross moments

∞

Sitting on the banks
Of a moonlit shore
Been given chances
To be granted
What should I ask of more?
That I may see you
For what you are?

For a moment
I find you

Only after
I lean against
That mirror
Impassioned
With my cheek and silhouette pressed against it
I don't see my own reflection
I see yours

And your hands
Perfectly grasped
Around my waist
One finger makes it
Up the small of my back
You hold my face

Eyes closed
I am awake
Dreaming
seeing clearly now

You line my neck with your nose tip
Trace your fingers over my bottom lip
Exhale Breath
Before the Kiss

My soul feel iridescent
Light pours and shatters the mirror
Where you once were
You are now gone

I am taken aback
Kneeling in the broken glass

And the moments cross over
Where I find myself in the sand

Sitting on the shores of those banks…

Life Is:

Life is love, love is immunity.
Life the beginning of ends to start again.
Life is the grounding and understanding of your purpose in the moment.
Life is the death of the old.
Life is courage to let go and freedom to move on.
Life is the balance of energy in vessels of flesh and bones.
Life is the infinite spectrum of vibrations and motivations.
Life is respect for all life forms.
Life: User discretion is advised.
Life is neither either or.
Life is currently undergoing metamorphosis.
Life is intending the future and living the moment.
Life is love. Love is the flow. Go with the flow.
Love is the undercurrent permeating consciousness.

Life is the inexplicable moments and catching glimpses into the unknown.
Fear is the antithesis of life.
Life is tireless and evermore.

Life is the infinite maze of unravelling of truth.
Life is knowing your power and using it wisely.

Life is knowing the longer I stay, the more trouble I have adjusting but realizing it all begins at the end of my comfort zone.

Like the universe, I am beautiful, complex, harmonious, conflicting.
I am a part of this universe and the universe is chaotic and constantly evolving.

Dare to be. Believe.
You must remain open to receive.
Life's mission is clear: make bonds, claim time, right wrongs, leave fear and love through to come through.

Missing

Do you miss something?
Someone?
What do you think you are missing?
An image?
An idea?
A moment?
A representation of the past? I

s it more complicated than that?
Maybe it is YOU you are missing.

Are you incomplete? Lonely? Think about it.

Or would you rather runaway and hide? Behind your pride? Or a glass? Or a smile? When really all of it is bound to shatter.

Not just you, but me too. We all have moments like that.
Don't apologize for being hard to understand.

View

Go On
Look Ahead
The Future in Now

With A Nod to The Past
I Realize How

Give Back

To know happiness
Is to know the secret
Never miss an opportunity
When you can seize it

Give back
Cause in the end
Your soul is full
Of what you left

Strength

My father once said

"You don't know your own strength"
Then I thought, not now, not yet
But its true though, you never do know
How strong you are
Until you've taken
A few blows...

Blindspot

Maintaining mystery
Drives me so crazy
But so does questioning love
Every time I look into the mirror
There you are in my blind spot

Tell me
What you want?

Futile Gaze

Life is too short for
Futile Gazes
Shallow or Appreciation
Or Seeking Validation
In these Ways

Letting Go

The difference between
Giving Up and
Letting Go
Is finding that space in between
And trusting that
What may
Or may not happen
Is meant to be

Polarities

To the calm and collected
To the chaotic and disruptive
To the shadow that leans toward my shoulder
To the light that never gets older

That never gave out
Even if I were out of breath
To the light that still guides
Most of my steps

To my demons inside that shame me
To the guidance that tries befriending

Now is all the time

Stay quiet
Do damage
Organize
Redefine
And love
That beautiful mess inside

www.ingramcontent.com/pod-product-compliance
Lightning Source LLC
Chambersburg PA
CBHW051748130826
49812CB00033B/1054
9789395784337